Jesus' Secret

What if his secret is better?

Doug Heisel

Jesus traveled across the galaxies
to share His secret with you.

What if His secret is better?

Table of Contents

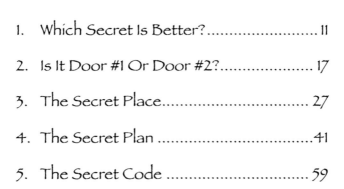

Acknowledgements

To all my dear friends who helped make, and continue to make, New Life Church such a joy to pastor. Life is better because I have the privilege of sharing the journey with you.

To my ministry mentors who I know personally, and others whose books and messages have inspired and shaped me. Harley and Kaye Allen, for believing in a young want-to-be minister, and then years later, believing in and supporting the vision of starting New Life Church. Your legacy continues. Bill Hybels and Andy Stanley, for how your ministries and messages have increased my desire and ability to communicate with people outside the walls of the church.

To my life-long friend, Greg Wingard. Like iron sharpens iron, so a friend sharpens a friend.

To both sets of parents (Heisels and Hardys). You were not only great parents to both me and Crystal; you were models of what true Christians are. Our foundation, as well as our life today, is blessed by you.

To my three wonderful girls (Joy, Rachel, and Emilie). You are truly gifts from God and are my three beautiful princesses. You make a dad proud.

To Crystal, my best friend, my wife, the outstanding mother to our kids, and my partner in ministry. I can't imagine life without you. You are the best! If I had it to do all over, I'd choose you again in a heartbeat. You have no equal. My life with you just gets better and better. I admire you, like you, and love you with all my heart! You make me better.

And to Jesus, who gave me His amazing grace I didn't deserve, love I can't comprehend, and power I can't exhaust. My life is changed forever. Thank You for sharing Your secrets with me!

Which Secret Is Better?

If you are like me, someone handed it to you and said something like, "You've got to check this out!" For me, it was a black DVD case with two prominent words written on it: *The Secret.* The subtitle read, "The Secret has traveled across the centuries to reach you." The packaging created curiosity as to what the big secret was and how it could have found me!

Over the next couple of weeks, several other people handed me additional copies of the DVD. Numerous times I was stopped and asked what I thought about the book. I've never seen that type of buzz on any other book or movie before. It was some kind of unorganized grassroots phenomenon.

It didn't take long though to figure out why it was taking place. Besides the intriguing packaging and expert guests, *The Secret*, in its simplest terms, addressed a question all of us have—"How do I get the things in life that I want?" *The Secret* claimed to finally have the answer.

What was held secret for hundreds and thousands of years by an elite few, was now being revealed to people like you and me. As the back of the books proclaims, *"You will come to know how you can have, be or do anything you want."*

I can come to know how I can have, be, or do anything I want? That sounds like the best deal anyone has ever made, doesn't it?

But what if there is a secret better than *The Secret*? In fact, what if Jesus has a secret?

What if Jesus has a secret that He not only is willing to reveal; what if His secret is better?

Picture this. Picture two doors.

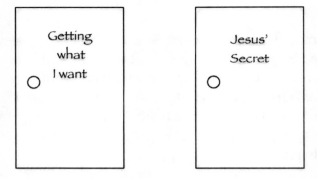

The door on your left says, "Getting what I want." The door on your right reads, "Jesus' Secret."

Over the next few pages, let's let those two doors represent two secrets — two doors to some kind of fulfillment. Let's set them side by side and examine some of their claims. Let's explore them, and then, you decide which one you would rather choose.

If you have read or watched *The Secret (or* know nothing about it) I dare you to explore Jesus' secret.

I dare
you to
explore
Jesus'
secret

Is it Door #1 or Door #2?

When I was a kid, there was a popular game show called, "Let's Make a Deal." If you are old enough to remember the show, you probably remember Monty Hall and Carol Merril. They were the host and assistant who gave hundreds of people a choice. The choice was to pick which door you thought had the most valuable gift behind it. Was it Door #1, Door #2, or Door #3? You could only pick one door. Only one door had the really valuable prize behind it. One door had a prize of moderate value. Then, one door had the cheap, goofy consolation prize that you probably couldn't sell at a garage sale.

The Secret appears to be a door that has the valuable prize behind it. Maybe it's the most valuable prize a person could ever acquire—the opportunity to have, be, or do anything you want.

The *secret* of *The Secret* is found in the Law of Attraction. This law is like a magnet to the universe. It is like a cosmic genie ready to give you whatever your mind and emotions focus on the most, positive or negative.

In many ways *The Secret* sounds a bit like prayer—with the mystery of unanswered prayer taken out. Instead of praying to God to get what I want, I simply focus on what I want, with enough passion and gratitude, and the universe delivers it into my life. Mystery and confusion gone.

My aim is to challenge our thinking and hopefully point to something better that many of us unintentionally may be missing.

In fact, I don't know if you caught this in *The Secret*, but not only has the mystery of prayer disappeared, so is this thing called "God's will for your life".

If you watched the DVD all the way to the end, or if you read the book to the back, you would have come across these words from one of the guest experts, Neale Donald Walsch. He said, "There is no blackboard in the sky on which God has written your purpose, your mission in life . . . your purpose is what you say it is. Your mission is the mission you give yourself. Your life will be what you create it as, and no one will stand in judgment of it, now or ever" (page 177).

A lineup of other guests then echo similar sentiments. The section culminated with these words: "Follow your bliss and the universe will open doors for you where there were only walls" (Joseph Campbell, The Secret, page 180).

As I said, picture two doors. But now, understand that picking the door that says "Getting what I want" may at the same time be saying, "There is no such thing as God or God's will for my life."

Are you ready to say that, or would you be willing to explore Jesus' secret first?

Let me throw out a question that I believe is one of life's key questions. How you answer this question will determine the trajectory of your entire life.

Here it is:

Is true fulfillment about <u>creating</u> the life I think I want or <u>discovering</u> the life I was created for?

Carefully read those words again; let them really sink in. Is true fulfillment about *creating* the life I think I want or *discovering* the life I was created for? Is it Door #1 or Door #2?

Those are two totally different ways to look at life! Do I attempt to *create* what I want through the Law of Attraction or through luck or hard work, or even through prayer (if I believe in God)? Is fulfillment more about *creating* or *discovering*? Is there a personal God who is at the center of everything—and does He have a plan for my life? Or, is it up to me and my limited perspective to determine the course and quality of my own life?

That question cuts right to the heart of *The Secret*, doesn't it?

It also cuts to the heart of prayer. What is the ultimate purpose of prayer? Is it to get something from God or is there a purpose even greater and more valuable than just getting what I want?

Think about prayer for a moment. If you pray, you probably don't remember the first prayer you ever prayed. But likely, if you did pray, it was a prayer that someone taught you.

Perhaps it was something like this one: "Now I lay me down to sleep, I pray the Lord my soul to keep. If I die before I wake, I pray the Lord my soul to take." Then, in my house, we would add a series of "Bless so and so and so and so. Amen." After that, you would climb into bed a little worried about whether or not this was the night you were going to die! Who made up the death prayer anyway?

There were bedtime prayers and mealtime prayers, and then, in my home, there were prayers for "traveling mercies." That was the official term we used, "traveling mercies" (plural).

We only prayed the traveling mercies prayer when we were taking a trip out of town. Apparently, in town we were already covered. But anytime we were going out of town on the highway, before we left, one of my parents would say, "Let's pray for traveling mercies."

This was back in the day when there were no special car seats for kids and no one wore seatbelts. My three siblings and I all played in the back of our blue station wagon. The seats folded down to make one big play area.

There was just a narrow windowpane between us and the eighteen wheelers that we were trying to get to honk their horns. No wonder we needed the traveling mercies prayer!

Now there is nothing wrong with praying for traveling mercies or for meals or for bedtime blessings. But here's the point. Somewhere along the line, regardless of how we were raised, most of our prayers wound up at the same destination. They wound up, basically, being about getting the things in life we wanted. They wound up at Door #1. I call them "Bless me—help me prayers."

I know many of us throw in a few interchangeable words like, "Give me . . . protect me . . . heal me." I know we often manage to work in a "thank You for the day" or something like it. But think about it (I've been guilty of this too) —don't most of our prayers boil down to, "Bless me, help me"?

Prayer for many people is merely the Christian version of *The Secret*. It is going to God to get through Door #1 (Getting what I want).

Then, for people who don't pray, or for people who gave up on praying, often the reason they stopped was because somewhere they prayed a "bless me, help me" prayer, and it didn't appear to work. They prayed it for themselves or for someone else, and nothing seemed to happen.

As a result, they concluded that prayer didn't work or God didn't care, or this thing was just too confusing. That dilemma many then have prompted them to look for something else.

For some, along came *The Secret* to provide an alternate way to get what they wanted. And basically, the mystery is taken out because fundamentally, life is all about the electrical impulses we send (or don't send) out to the universe. The universe is essentially described like a giant cosmic vending machine, a genie ready to grant your every wish, if you just learn to get in harmony with it (The Secret, page 45, 46) . If you learn how to place your order correctly, you can have or be whatever you want.

What if there is something more important than merely getting the things in life I think I want or need? As improbable as the will first appear, what if Door #2 (the Jesus' secret door) is truly better?

Please don't misunderstand me. My aim is not to bash a book or DVD or any of those who contributed to it. I accept that their intent is to genuinely try to help people. Besides, some of their material (like the value of gratitude, the need to take responsibility verses acting and thinking like a victim) is great.

Furthermore, it is not my desire to criticize the way many of us pray. My aim is to humbly challenge our thinking and point to something Jesus offered that many of us have missed.

Think about this. What if there is something more important than merely getting the things in life I think I want or need? As improbable as that will first appear, what if Door #2 (Jesus' Secret) is truly better? What if it represents the words recorded in the Bible, in the book of Ephesians? It says this: **"God can do anything, you know—far more than you could ever imagine or guess or request in your wildest dreams! He does it not by pushing us around but by working within us, his Spirit deeply and gently within us"** (Ephesians 3:20 The Message).

Is there a life better than my limited imagination and perspective? Am I actually able to manipulate the universe with my mood swings? Or is there a powerful God who has a plan for my life? Is it cosmic energy I align my life with or is there something else — some One else who designed me with a purpose? Is there some One else who designed <u>you</u> with a purpose?

Let me ask the question again. Is life ultimately about *creating,* or is it about *discovering*?

I am glad you have joined me as we explore that important question. Let's take a walk over to Door #2. Let's explore Jesus' Secret. After that, you decide which door you think has the better offer behind it. Is it Door #1 or Door #2?

Is true fulfillment about
creating the life
I think I want, or discovering
the life
I was created for?

The Secret Place

Once you have seen it, you never forget it. A few of us have seen it, but all of us have likely heard about it. This spectacle has become an idiom of our day.

When something is running around kind of crazy—kind of disjointed—doing nothing productive or constructive, we often say it's like a chicken with his head cut off.

When I was a kid, I lived on a farm in northern Minnesota. We didn't have chickens, but one of our neighboring farmers did. I don't know how it happened but when I saw it, it was kind of funny, kind of scary and kind of sad.

It was kind of funny because of how crazy it looked. There was a chicken body, with chicken feathers and chicken legs, and it was running around, but there was *no* chicken head! At least not one that was attached.

It was also kind of scary because there was a chicken running around with *no* head! How long would it keep running? Could it see me laughing at it? If it could run with no head, what other terrible things was it capable of doing? Could it show up in my room in the middle of the night? It was kind of scary.

But mostly, it was kind of sad because it was dead except that all of its parts hadn't been informed!

Do you ever feel like that? Ever feel like you are running around with your head missing?

I wonder how it looks from God's perspective. I bet some of it looks kind of funny. "Look at what they are trying to do down there!" It probably looks kind of scary: "What are they thinking?" But mostly, I bet it looks kind of sad. "It doesn't have to be like this; there is a better way."

There really is a better way. I am delighted you have decided to explore your options. Door #1 is hard to pull away from.

Grab hold of your head and walk with me now to Door #2. Let's begin to discover what I am calling "Jesus' Secret", and specifically, in this chapter, something we might even call "Jesus' Secret Place." It's His antidote to running around with our heads cut off.

Let's read a passage from the Bible and then take a few minutes to highlight and think about what Jesus is offering us.

What if there is something much greater than just more "Bless me, help me"?

The passage begins in Matthew 6:5. These are the verses that lead up to the well known prayer which we call The Lord's Prayer. These verses set the stage (the context) for that prayer.

Many of us know the Lord's Prayer —the, *"Our Father who art in heaven, hallowed be thy name"* prayer.

Many of us can quote the Lord's Prayer. But most of us have no idea what Jesus said about prayer right before He gave us that prayer.

Here's what He said about prayer before the big prayer. This is part of Jesus' secret: ***"And when you pray, do not be like the hypocrites"*** *(vs. 5).*

Jesus begins by essentially saying, "You want to learn about prayer? Let me teach you something about prayer because the people who are most visible, the people who you might be watching, are doing it *wrong!*"

Wrong? That sounds kind of harsh. Isn't prayer just talking to God? Can't we do that any way we want?

Well, apparently not if you know what Jesus knows about prayer. You see, part of Jesus' secret involves understanding some things about prayer. Before Jesus begins telling us *how* to pray, He tells us how *not* to pray!

"And when you pray, do not be like the hypocrites . . . for they love to pray standing in the synagogues and on the street corners to be seen by men."

The first thing Jesus tells us about prayer has to do with *where* we do it.

Now, isn't that kind of odd? I thought you could pray anywhere! I thought you could pray driving down the freeway while putting on makeup or reviewing the notes for a test or some big proposal you have to make.

"God help me pass my test . . . God help me clinch this deal . . . Oh God, don't let that police officer pull me over!"

"God, make her call me back. God, make him stop calling me! Help me, bless me!"

I think you can pray anywhere, any time. In fact, I'm a huge promoter of learning to have conversations with God throughout the day.

I think that's one of the first things to learn about prayer—that it is available anytime, anywhere. This is not a prohibition against all public prayers. Instead, it is more of an invitation to experience something that cannot and does not happen in public. It is an invitation to understand prayer the way Jesus understands prayer. And the first area He deals with is *where*.

"Do not be like the hypocrites, for they love to pray standing in the synagogues and on the street corners to be seen by men. I tell you the truth, they have received their reward" *(vs. 5).*

Say those last two words again—*their reward.*

"They have received their reward in full. " (vs. 5)

In other words, this kind of prayer has some reward attached to it. Their motive, apparently, was to be seen. Jesus said, "You were seen! Good job. You prayed. People saw you. Enjoy that reward."

We might take it a step further and say, if all prayer is done in public, or in church, or on the run—whenever and where ever—there is some kind of *reward* to that. God hears those prayers.

Furthermore, there are times we are challenged and encouraged to pray with other people. Matthew 18:19 talks about two people agreeing together in prayer. The book of James encourages group prayer for the sick (James 5:14). We are even prompted to share prayerful confession with at least one other person (James 5:16). Some forms of prayer are actually better with other people.

But listen. Jesus is going to tell us that something very important and very powerful will only happen when you are *not* praying in public or *not* praying on the run. It's almost as if He is saying, "You want to know a secret? Then listen up!"

"But when you pray, go into your room and close the door" *(vs. 6).*

Go into the place behind Door #2, (Jesus' Secret), and find a room. It doesn't have to be some specific one-of-a-kind type of room specifically designed for praying. We know that because we don't really have any stories of Jesus praying by Himself in a room. His room was on a mountaintop, in the olive grove, or out in the wilderness. I actually prefer an air-conditioned room to the wilderness, but the point is, Jesus' first secret is to get a place where you are alone with your Heavenly Father.

This is a place where you are not multi-tasking, not on the run, and not with other people. Those prayers have some benefit and some reward, but if you want to know Jesus' Secret, He says, "Find a place where it is just you and your Father, who is unseen—and go there and close the door behind you."

Because (catch this): *"Then your Father, who sees what is done in secret will reward you! (vs. 6).*

The first part is not about *a secret*, it is about being *in secret*. It is about being one on one with the God who made you, the God who wants to reconnect with you as your Heavenly Father. If you do that, there is a reward behind that door.

The first part of Jesus' Secret is not about a secret, it is about being in secret.

Now that's what I'm talking about! Finally, we get to where it's about *me!* God is going to give me what I want. That's the reward, right?

Wait a minute! What if the reward Jesus is speaking about is much more valuable than merely getting what I want? What if there is something so much better than more "Bless me, help me"? And what if the reward comes out of a private time between me and God?

Let me illustrate it this way. If the only conversation I have with my wife, Crystal, is on the go, how rich will our relationship be? Will we experience life to the fullest, if all we do is talk about things like: who's picking up who . . . what's for dinner . . . what's on the agenda, what needs to be fixed, or the all important — what stuff do we want to buy . . . and have — ? If that's all we do, even if we do it in style (the right house, the right cars, the right toys), could we wake up one day feeling disconnected? Couldn't we wind up saying something like, "I'm not really happy. I don't know if I really know you!"?

Is a marriage really rich if it is not rich relationally? Can you have all the right stuff and still not be happy? I think you know the answer to that as well as I do!

That is why, even though raising our kids has been away from Grandma and Grandpa, we still found capable loving people to take our kids for a couple of hours (even when they were babies). We found time to get in the car and *close the door behind us* to go out on a date night. That's why every year (even though we love our kids, in fact, because we love our kids) we get in the car or head to the airport. The *door closes behind us,* and it's just the two of us heading somewhere to be by ourselves. Something happens relationally during that time together that doesn't happen when we are with the kids.

> Fulfillment doesn't come by simply getting more stuff. It will not, and cannot, bring you what your soul is really craving deep down inside.

When our kids are with us, I call it a family trip. When I am alone with Crystal, I call it a vacation! There's a huge difference.

This is also why, almost every night, it is my ritual to kick our kids out of our room; I close the door and lock it. Close, intimate relationships cannot be done on the fly—only focusing on what we need or want to have. That's part of life, but it's just a small part of what makes people feel fulfilled. Intimacy doesn't happen in public. Fulfillment doesn't come by simply getting more stuff.

You probably know where this is going, don't you? Jesus is challenging us to consider stepping away from Door #1 to experience something far greater, something He calls a reward. And that reward is going to come out of a secret place where I slow down long enough to really connect with a God who Jesus calls "your Heavenly Father."

But what about my needs and wants? What about the problems I have that I need God's help with?

Look at this—Jesus adds this in verse 7: *"And when you pray, do not keep on babbling like pagans, for they think they will be heard* [that means, taken more seriously] *because of their many words."*

If you come from an unchurched background and you are a little afraid of what to say, or unsure of what to say, to the Father, Jesus takes the pressure off you right from the beginning! He wants you to understand that the Father is not moved by the volume, the quantity, or even the so-called quality of some words over other words. That's not the issue. In fact, too many words (babbling) seem to be part of the problem.

So Jesus says in verse 8, *"Do not be like them."*

Then He says, *"For your Father knows what you need before you ask him."*

Read that again: *"For your Father knows what you need before you ask him."*

What Jesus is saying is this: God cares about what you need and want. He cares about Door #1. But listen. It is as if Jesus is saying, "The thing you are so focused on, that thing you think is the big deal, it is really just a small corner compared to what the real deal, the big reward, really is" (Door #2).

God already knows about Door #1. Door #1 is important. It's fine; we'll talk about going through Door #1 in chapter 5. But Jesus is really saying, "Door #1 by itself is *not* the real deal. It will not, and cannot, bring you what your soul is craving deep down inside."

What if the real deal is behind Door #2? What if the *better secret*, the *true secret*, is not first and foremost about *getting*? What if it is about *discovering*? And what if that discovery comes out of a private time between you and your Heavenly Father? Would you be willing to consider that? Would you be willing to try this instead?

What if you did this first? What if you carved out some time and decided on a secret place where you actually developed an authentic and intimate relationship with your Heavenly Father? Then, what if you came to realize that all the stuff you are worried about, all the stuff you want,

What if there really is a God who has a <u>plan</u> for your life? And what if ultimate fulfillment comes from discovering Him and it?

all the stuff you need, all the stuff you have been trying to attract into your life (or pray into your life) are all things your Heavenly Father already knows and cares about? After fully comprehending that, you begin to realize how small that stuff is compared to what He wants to do for you when you get a secret place where you are alone with Him.

Now I understand what you might be thinking. "I'm going to go into some room and close the door and something really important is going to happen to me? Are you serious?" You might then add this thought to the previous one. "And if I go in there and close the door, and it is not about my needs and my desires, what in the world am I supposed to be doing in there?"

Well, that's the next chapter! Before we get there, will you let this idea sink into your mind?

You could make the rest of your life about figuring out the formula for getting stuff (Door #1). You could be counting on the right prayer formula or the right Law of Attraction formula. But what if along the way of doing that, you missed out on the richer, deeper, bigger reward?

What if the real secret was to discover an intimate connection with your Heavenly Father, where you begin to understand what He created you to have, do and become?

What if there really is a God who has a plan for your life? What if ultimate fulfillment comes from discovering Him and it? Wouldn't you want that?

One day Jesus stopped, after watching people rush about doing all the stuff they were doing. He watched the religious people doing their religious stuff. As he watched them, I wonder how much it looked to Him like my sad chicken story.

He stopped and essentially said, "Can I let you in on a secret? There's something you are missing, something that will never come any other way, something that is bigger than just getting the stuff you think you need and want. But it all begins by understanding the importance of having a secret place where you go and close the door behind you."

I know for some of us this could sound really strange. You might be thinking you are hearing the "Twilight Zone" music playing in the background. But just pause a moment and consider this. Is it possible to spend your entire life striving for something and yet miss the most important thing? I think so.

What if you were created to know God — to know Him as a Heavenly Father? Then, what if, in that relationship, you discovered His plan for your life, a plan that can certainly involve stuff, but goes way beyond just getting what I want (Door #1).

I think we would all do well to wrestle with the life question I opened this book with:

"Is ultimate fulfillment about creating the life I think I want, or is it about discovering the life I was created for?"

If you are beginning to sense that it is the latter, perhaps you will want to embrace, or renew, a spiritual declaration like this: **"I will daily slow down for some private and personal time with my Heavenly Father."**

I believe there is a God who loves you. I believe He has a great plan for your life. Part of that plan (maybe the biggest part) is to connect with you in a way that you don't simply know about Him — you know Him. When you know Him, there is a reward in that which dwarfs all other things.

Is your life right now so busy, so fast-paced, that it's hard to slow down? I encourage you – I challenge you – to start with this. Write this declaration down (or go to our website where you can download and print a nice copy: www. JesusSecretBook.com.) Post it in a prominent place where you see it throughout the day. Let the concept sink in before you attempt to implement it. Begin to change your thinking before you endeavor to change your habits.

One simple way to do that is to begin to mentally remind yourself of what you are learning and what you will begin to soon do.

Jesus begins with the importance of a secret place before He shares His secret plan. I encourage you to begin there too!

Spiritual Declaration #1

"I will daily slow down for some private and personal time with my Heavenly Father."

Secret Summaries

- How you answer this question will determine the trajectory of your entire life:

  Is true fulfillment about *creating* the life I think I want or *discovering* the life I was created for?

- Discovery of what I was created for emerges from a secret place where I slow down and spend some personal and private time with my Heavenly Father.

Valuable Action Step

If you don't have a specific place and time to get alone with your Heavenly Father, make plans today to do that. Pick a place and then determine what time you will show up there tomorrow. Like any other important event, put it on your calendar. Do this every day for the next ninety days. Determine one day in advance when the best time will be to show up there tomorrow. Start off with just ten minutes and let it grow and develop from there.

The Secret Plan

My wife Crystal and I have three children—three girls. Joy is the oldest, then Rachel, and finally Emilie (Emilie with an "ie" not a "y"—as she will quickly tell you).

As delightful as they are, all three girls did something that I also did as a kid. I bet you did it too. As a matter of fact, every child on the planet has likely done it.

Somewhere between one and two years of age a phrase develops. No parent ever taught their child to say it—but it doesn't matter. Somehow, it mysteriously winds up in the vocabulary of every preschool aged child.

To my best recollection, with all three of my girls, the phrase was said in conjunction with clothing.

These babies, who needed my help so badly the day before, woke up one morning and, one by one, informed me that they no longer needed my assistance. I believe the exact phrase was, "No Daddy! I'll do it myself!"

Now don't get me wrong; ultimately, I wanted my children to learn to dress themselves. Certainly I wanted them to learn to be responsible. But the first time you hear the phrase "No Daddy! I'll do it myself" is still a bit hard to take.

Hearing a child say those words is really not the problem. The problem with that phrase is this—it seems we never really let it leave our vocabulary. Throughout our entire lives, many of us (in one form or another) say to our Heavenly Father, "No Daddy! I'll do it myself."

Now, our Heavenly Father ultimately wants us to grow and be responsible, but He also knows we were never created to be independent of Him. He never taught us to say, "No Daddy! I'll do it myself."

That's where Jesus' Secret comes in. Jesus, more than anyone, understands how dependant we are on our Heavenly Father. Therefore, He gave us a secret so we could experience something in our lives that will come no other way.

In the last chapter we talked about how Jesus begins to reveal His secret. We were imagining a door (Door #2) with the words *"Jesus' Secret"* written on it.

Jesus invited us to begin this adventure by first going through that door to discover and establish a secret place.

He said, *"But when you pray, go into your room, close the door and pray to your Father, who is*

> Discovering the life I was created for comes out of this kind of private and personal time with God.

unseen. Then your Father, who sees what is done in secret, will reward you" (Matthew 6:6).

It is as if Jesus is saying, "If you want to understand fulfillment, if you want to take your life to an entirely new level, then you have to take some time where you break away from other people. You have to slow down for some private and personal time with your Heavenly Father. You have to go into a room and close the door."

Discovering the life I was created for comes out of this kind of private and personal time with God. It is forged behind a closed door when I get one on one with my Heavenly Father.

The first part of Jesus' Secret was not a secret, but a secret place. Better yet, it wasn't a secret, it was being in secret — being alone, where it is just you and God.

"Then your Father, who sees what is done in secret, will reward you" (vs. 6).

I first begin with a commitment to a time and place alone with God. But once I go in the room—if the point isn't all about what I need and want—what's left? What am I going to pray about? What am I going to do in the room if it's not all about me?

That is exactly what Jesus reveals next. Let's call it "Jesus' Secret Plan." It is not only a plan for discovering God's will for your life, but a plan for you to experience a deeper and richer relationship with your Heavenly Father (which might just be what, deep down inside, your soul craves and needs more than anything else).

Do you know what is so amazing about His secret plan? He figured out a way for most of us to already have it memorized. Does that surprise you? If you didn't memorize the plan, you most likely have heard the plan multiple times before. You've just never unlocked the secret behind the plan.

Can you memorize something and not really get it? Can someone memorize the Pledge of Allegiance and miss its meaning? Can someone memorize a speed limit sign, and pretty much ignore it? If you live in California, like I do, it would appear that speed limit signs are more "speed suggestion" signs. We see the number, we might even memorize it, but mostly "speed limit 65" pretty much gets ignored where I live.

What's going to surprise many of us is that we have already memorized Jesus' Secret Plan. But like some speed limit signs, we don't really follow what we have memorized.

Now, just in case you don't believe that you already know the plan (possibly even have memorized the plan), go ahead and read it. See if it sounds familiar to you.

"Our Father in heaven, hallowed be your name, your kingdom come, your will be done on earth as it is in heaven. Give us today our daily bread. Forgive us our debts, as we also have forgiven our debtors. And lead us not into temptation, but deliver us from the evil one."

Could it be that a <u>secret plan</u> has been hidden in plain sight all these years and many of us have missed it?

OK, haven't you heard that prayer somewhere? You might even be someone who has it pretty well memorized. But here's the deal: do you realize that Jesus never gave us this prayer to memorize? It was never intended to be some magic religious words that we mechanically recite, hoping for something miraculous to happen. It is not a mantra to mimic; it's a pattern to follow. It is a plan to use as a guide – a guide that has three parts. Unfortunately, two of those parts most of us have totally ignored or missed.

Could it be that a secret plan has been hidden in plain sight all these years and many of us have missed it? Can something be right in front of you and you not see it?

Who hasn't lost their car keys, only to discover they are lying on the kitchen counter right in plain view? It is easy to miss what is right in front of you.

When I suggest that many of us have memorized Jesus' secret plan but have missed seeing it, that shouldn't be hard to fathom. It doesn't have to stay that way.

Jesus not only wants you to see the plan; what if following the plan could unlock rewards that the "getting what I want" door (Door #1) alone could never do? I think it can.

Let me pause and say this before we look at the plan.

Some of us will be tempted to dismiss this "Secret Plan" because it will appear to be too simple to be significant. Some of us will be tempted to dismiss the plan for another reason that I think you will see on your own in the pages to follow. But, hopefully you will be one of those individuals who will choose to follow the plan — and when you do, it could become the most important plan you ever follow.

Let's break this down. Jesus essentially said, "Go into a room and close the door behind you. Then, before you get to all your needs, wants, wishes, and questions (that I already know about anyway) here's what I want you to do. This will begin to unlock a secret passageway between Me and you."

Then, notice how Jesus begins His prayer. Read the first line again: *"Our Father in heaven, hallowed be your name."*

When I pray my kind of prayer (bless me, help me), who am I beginning with — me or God? My kind of prayer begins with me. For some strange reason, Jesus appears to have a problem with that!

When Jesus gives us His prayer (His plan) who does He begin with - me or God? *God.* And it's not just a salutation line like, "Dear God, here's what's on my wish list today."

Beginning with God doesn't just mean we start by saying His name, like we are trying to get His attention! "Dear God, it's me. Doug. Hello! Could You turn some of Your attention my way? I have some important stuff I'd like You to do for me!"

No, the emphasis of Jesus' prayer is on the *"Hallowed be Your name"* part.

Do you know the word used in the rest of the Bible for "hallowed be your name?" The action word that describes what it means when Jesus says, "hallowed be your name" is the word "worship."

If you want to really pray—not just that little corner where it's about what you want—if you want to unlock some secret passages between you and God, then you have to start with God. You have to start by comprehending and declaring who you are going to be talking with.

Picture this: picture going through Jesus' Secret door (Door #2). It's a corner of your bedroom or a quiet place in your house where you are alone. Try and pick some place or some chair you normally don't use for other things. Let it become a place you associate with connecting with God. As ordinary or unsanctified as that place may be (like a closet or spot in the garage) it can become a holy place for you.

When you get there, slow down and say something like I do almost every morning: *"Father, before I do anything else, I want to once again remind myself how big and great and holy and compassionate and generous You are."*

I often repeat those words to let them fully sink in.

As I begin to do that (even though I am not Italian) I feel like I need to use my hands. Most of the time I simply turn them palms up or I raise them up—and instead of words I use my hands as an expression of my openness to His presence. I use them as a sign of my adoration of His worthiness. I use them as a sign that I desire to connect with my Heavenly Father. I learned this from my kids.

When my kids were young, all three of them (without prompting) did an interesting thing. When they wanted to be picked up, they stood and looked up, and said only one word. Every parent knows the word. The child just looks up and says, "Up!" Just "up." It's not even a complete sentence! But all parents know exactly what their child wants. Not so much because of the word "up", as much as the position of their hands. What position were their hands in? Up.

Try that sometime with God. When you need Him the most, open your hands and your heart, and with the simplicity of a child learn to say "up". That can be one of the simplest forms of worship.

Often, for me, the fewer the words the better. It becomes a few moments of silent worship where I get still and know that He is God.

However you do this, the key is to learn to shut out everything else and remind yourself who you are connecting with.

Worship is our gateway into God's presence. Say that out loud, will you? Worship is our gateway into God's presence.

It is as if it unlocks a secret door, an invisible door, between my room and His room.

I realize that some people won't do this because of pride or ego. It might sound silly or

Worship is

our

gateway

into God's

presence.

spooky to others. But will you at least consider this fact? Worship is all throughout the Bible. For those of us who will stretch ourselves and learn about worshipping God in private, worship will become our gateway into God's presence.

Now, the point of this book is not primarily about worship or how to be a better worshipper. There are other great books for that. My aim here is to simply point out what Jesus begins His secret plan with. He begins not with my wishes, dreams, or needs. He begins with the ultimate first-things-first—God. He begins with the most important relationship I will ever have, my relationship with my Heavenly Father.

But, Jesus isn't finished yet. Worship opens the door; it brings me into God's presence, but this next secret opens my heart and mind to His plan.

Let's go back to the Lord's Prayer. Here's the next phrase. It says, *"Your kingdom come, your will be done on earth as it is in heaven."*

Before God even begins to reveal His plan to me, He expects me to surrender to it first.

Check out what is happening. This is another part of Jesus' Secret that many people will not do. Before God begins to reveal His plan to me, He expects me to surrender to it <u>first</u>!

He wants us to say something on a regular basis. It's a central part of His secret plan. It might sound something like this: "Father, you are a good God. You know what's best, better than I know what's best. So, whatever Your will is, whatever role You want me to play in Your kingdom—before I know what that is—I accept it. Let Your kingdom dominate my kingdom; let Your will dominate my will. Do it in my life, on this earth just like it happens in heaven."

That's one of the greatest secrets you and I need to know about God. **He does not reveal His will to those who have not first surrendered theirs.** And He wants us to surrender to Him (and to it), without even knowing what *it* is!

That's why worship is first. In worship, we begin to more fully comprehend who God is. When that happens, we begin to encounter Him and begin to see how He can be fully trusted. When we fully trust, surrender is not hard at all – it is the natural outflow.

Jesus' Secret to knowing God and His plan is called "surrender." It is daily putting God's will ahead of my own.

Instead of declaring to a universe what I want for my life, I surrender to the God who created me. I surrender my will to His:

(Your kingdom come, Your will be done on earth as it is in heaven.)

Before I get to my needs and wants (Door #1), before I get to where I pray about my daily bread, or receiving more of His forgiving and empowering grace, Jesus' Secret Plan has at its core the word "surrender."

I don't totally understand how this works, but I do know this – my ability to hear God's still small voice is directly related to my willingness to surrender. It's not a physical voice that my physical ear hears. This is spiritual and it requires something deeper than that physical. It is a spiritual voice to my spiritual ear. Believe it or not, all of us have one!

> Instead of declaring to a universe what I want for my life, I surrender to the God who created me.

Anytime I begin my day with worship and surrender – anytime I sit quietly before the Lord and do these two things, my ability to discern God's voice grows, and my ability to sense His leading grows. Anytime I do those two things, the next step He wants me to take becomes clearer.

These two words are Jesus' Secret Plan to take your relationship with your Heavenly Father to the level God wants. It's His secret plan to tune us into His agenda for our lives.

In the next chapter we'll talk about the third part of Jesus' secret plan—"receiving." This is where we actually go back to Door #1 (Getting what I want). But when we go back, we go back different.

Before we go there though, will you camp on these two words a while? Will you let the significance and power of these two steps sink deep into your heart and mind? They are far more important than most of us realize.

Worship   Surrender

Let me wrap them up into a sentence—a second spiritual declaration. This is something you can hang on your mirror and review every morning until it becomes a vital part of you life.

Spiritual Declaration #2:

"I will discover the life I was created for by growing in my worship of my Heavenly Father; surrendering, in advance, to His will, and receiving from Him all He promises to give."

That is Jesus' prayer – His secret plan in a sentence.

Before you go on to the next chapter, perhaps you could turn the first two parts of that declaration into your own prayer. Consider praying something like I pray. Let me give it to you one more time:

"Father, I remind myself how big, great, holy, compassionate and generous You are."

Then I pause, and really let those words sink in. I close my eyes and let my heart and mind truly embrace the significance of what I just said. I lift my hands toward heaven and I pause, even if just for a few moments. I don't say another word. I just put into practice what the psalmist learned thousands of years ago, "Be still, and know that He is God!" (Psalm 46:10).

After that, I say this: "I surrender again to Your will. Your will and way is the only way to true life and freedom. It is Your kingdom that matters and Your will that needs to be done in and through my life today. Lead and direct me throughout this day. "

Those two steps, prayed every day, have made a tremendously positive impact on my life. Instead of telling the universe what I want, my Heavenly Father, the shepherd of my soul *"leads me in paths of righteousness for his name's sake"* (Psalm 23:3). What a comfort to know someone infinitely wiser and more powerful than me is personally guiding my life.

When I have taken those two steps, they prepare me for the next step—receiving from Him all He promises to give!

We are now ready to come back to Door #1.

Spiritual Declaration #2:

"I will discover the life I
was created for by
growing in my worship
of my Heavenly Father;
surrendering, in advance,
to His will; and receiving
from Him all He
promises to give."

Secret Summaries

- Although our Heavenly Father ultimately wants us to grow and be responsible, He knows we were never created to be independent of Him. He never taught us to say, "No Daddy! I'll do it myself."

- Worship is our gateway into God's presence. It is as if it unlocks a secret door between my room and His room.

- Instead of declaring to the universe what I want for my life, I surrender to the God who created me. I surrender my will to His.

- Before God begins to reveal His plan to me, He expects me to surrender to Him and his plan first.

Valuable Action Step

Spiritual declarations can be great reminders of what we have learned; but more importantly, they can begin to focus us where we want to go. We move towards what we daily focus on. Tear out the "Spiritual Declarations" page in the back of this book, or download a copy of it (www.JesusSecretBook. com). Hang it on the mirror you use to get ready in the morning. Recite the declarations out loud. Commit them to memory. Breakthrough behavior requires breakthrough beliefs. These declarations can help that happen.

The Secret Code

When you were a kid, did you ever have a fort or a club-house where you needed to know a secret code to get in? Maybe you would knock twice and pause; knock once and pause; then knock three more times. Then your buddies inside would recognize the code, unlock the door, and let you in. You had access because you knew the code.

What if Jesus has a code for receiving things from Him? What if that code involves knocking on a door in a certain way that the door opens to you?

I want to take you to an important story in the Bible. It is a similar passage to the one we have looked at already, but it is a different story, a different time, and it contains an additional insight into Jesus' Secret.

The story is found in the book of Luke. In chapter 11 it says, **"One day Jesus was praying in a certain place. When he finished, one of his disciples said to him, 'Lord, teach us to pray, just as John taught his disciples.'"**

Apparently this disciple saw Jesus praying by Himself. Jesus' secret place was often in a garden, so perhaps he actually watched Jesus pray. Maybe Jesus appeared to be doing something different, or maybe it was the answers to prayer that Jesus got that prompted this request. We don't know this disciple's motive for his request, but it is certainly reasonable to assume he was a lot like many of us. He wanted to know the code. He appears to be saying, "What do we have to do to get the results You get? How do we get through Door #1?"

What's interesting is Jesus' response. Instead of Jesus saying something like, "Come on. There is nothing to it. Prayer is just talking to God. Just say or do whatever you want."

No, instead of saying that, Jesus gave them a plan. He said to them (and to us), **"When you pray, say: 'Father, hallowed be your name, your kingdom come. Give us each day our daily bread. Forgive us our sins, for we also forgive everyone who sins against us. And lead us not into temptation.'"**

Now you might be thinking, "Yeah, we already learned that prayer. Except, you messed up the prayer. You left out some words. You didn't say Jesus' prayer the right way!"

No, remember that Jesus never gave us the prayer to memorize and mechanically say back to God. It was a pattern—a plan with three parts. This time there are a few less words, but Jesus gives us the same plan.

As you can see, this passage has the same three parts, just like the other passage. There is:

- **Worshipping God** (Father, hallowed be Your name).
- **Surrendering to His will** (Your kingdom come).
- **Receiving from Him those things we need**: food, forgiveness, direction and power. (Give us each day our daily bread. Forgive us our sins . . . lead us not into temptation...).

But, notice this. In the previous passage, Jesus gave us some additional teaching on prayer <u>before</u> He gave us the three principles of the Lord's Prayer. He gave us the significance of the secret place.

This time He gives us additional teaching on prayer, but it is <u>after</u> the Lord's Prayer. I'm calling this the "Secret Code." It's like an inside track on the receiving part of His prayer.

This time Jesus tells a parable, which is a story with a message. Here's what Jesus said:

"Suppose one of you has a friend, and he goes to him at midnight and says, 'Friend, lend me three loaves of bread, because a friend of mine on a journey has come to me, and I have nothing to set before him.' Then the one inside answers, 'Don't bother me.'" (That's Aramaic for, "Who in the world is bugging me at this time of night? Go away!")

"'The door is already locked, and my children are with me in bed. I can't get up and give you anything.'"

Let me push the pause button on the story a moment to provide some cultural background. When Jesus is telling this story, there were primarily two classes of people – rich and poor. Many poor people lived in one or two-room houses. One of the rooms was the sleeping room for the entire family. Everyone slept on mats on the floor in the same room. It was kind of like camping in a tent. If one person gets up and turns on a light, everybody is awake!

So the guy inside is saying, "Shhhh! Come on! What is the deal? Go away!"

Do you get the picture? If so, let's push "play", because the story is not over.

"I tell you, though he will not get up and give him the bread because he is his friend, yet because of the man's boldness he will get up and give him as much as he needs."

In other words, the guy is not going away. You can picture the scene in your mind. "Hey buddy, I need something. I need you to get up and help me. Come on. I know

63

you're in there. I can see you though the keyhole in the door. Come on! I can keep this pounding up all night if you want me to. Better come help me or you better have a good pair of ear plugs, because I haven't even begun to knock as loud as I can!"

That's why Jesus said, "I tell you, though he will not get up and give him the bread because he is his friend, he will get up because of the man's boldness." The word boldness is often translated "persistence". It literally means unashamed persistence.

If you have kids, you can relate to what this word means. See if this sounds familiar.

"Mom . . . Mom . . . Mom . . . Mom . . . Mom. . . "

They are like little machine guns shooting out mom bullets! Who taught them to do that? And how long will they keep doing it? As long as it takes! They will keep it up until mom stops what she is doing and says, "What?!"

Now get this: Mom doesn't stop because this is her child who she loves and adores. She stops because of what? She stops because of the unashamed relentless persistence of this kid!

By now, the disciples had been traveling with Jesus long enough to know how these stories generally work. Jesus tells a story and in the story someone represents them and often someone represents God. They begin to do the calculating. "Let's see. This story is about prayer, so the guy pounding on the door asking for help must be us. That makes God . . . that makes God the guy who is sleeping and doesn't want to be bothered?!"

Is Jesus saying that when I need help I have to first wake up God? I know many of us have felt that way at times, but is Jesus indicating that it is actually that way? Is that the secret code? Bang on the door to wake God up?

Thankfully, Jesus interprets His own story by the application He gives His disciples.

Jesus says, *"So I say to you: ask and it will be given to you; seek and you will find; knock and the door will be opened to you. For everyone who asks receives; he who seeks finds; and to him who knocks, the door will be opened."*

Thank goodness, the focus of Jesus' story is not on the guy sleeping. The focus of the story is on the specific bold persistence of the person asking.

It is as if Jesus is saying this about receiving things from God. If you really want to understand a key to prayer and getting things you want, do it this way. Just like sleeping-don't-bother-me kinds of friends are moved by specific and unashamed bold persistence, so is God moved by that! If you have something so specific, so big, and so important, you are willing to ask-seek-and knock ... and ask and seek and knock ... and ask and seek and knock, Jesus informs us how that moves the heart and hand of God!

Your Heavenly Father is not put off by big, bold, persistent prayers. They honor Him! They recognize the kind of God He is.

God is not just the mealtime God. He is not just the traveling mercies God. He is not just the help me pass my test, help me find a parking spot, or help me get a date God.

He is the kind of God who already knows about all of that and cares about all of that. Yes, go ahead and pray about those things. The last part of the Lord's Prayer does involve asking for His provision, forgiveness, direction, and power (Give us each day our daily bread. Forgive us our sins . . . lead us not into temptation).

Take some time to admit your need of His help, even with the smallest of items. But do it with this understanding—all those things are pretty much a given for a Father who cares about you.

Receive them. By faith, open your heart and life to receive what your Heavenly Father already knows you need.

Don't make asking for the basics the major focus of your prayer time. In Jesus' Sermon on the Mount, He told us not to go around worrying about those kinds of things (Matthew 6:25-34).

This parable goes beyond our daily needs. It is almost as if Jesus is saying, "Now that the basic stuff is covered, what do you really need and want? What is really important?"

Consider this. When was this guy doing his persistent pounding? It was the middle of the

What if a key to Door #1 (Getting what I want) is to identify one specific need or desire that tops all the others?

night! But this need, this thing he wanted, was so important he was willing to give up sleep for it!

Do you have any prayers so big, so important, so specific, you are willing to give up sleep for them?

Let me narrow this down even more. What if a key to Door #1 (Getting what I want) is to identify one specific need or desire that tops all the others? What if Jesus is teaching something about prayer that many of us have missed our entire lives? What if, out of all the things we think we need and want, we narrow it down to one thing that is so important, so big, and so central that all other things are secondary to it at that time? Then, what if learning to bring that one thing to God day after day in specific bold persistence is like a secret code most of us have missed?

Picture it this way. See yourself behind Door #2, in your secret place. Start by becoming intimately acquainted with who God is and what His kingdom is really like. Do this so that when it is time to focus on Door #1 (Get what I want), you are clearer than ever before on one thing you need or want from God. It needs to be something so big and important that you will be willing to bring it up day after day, even month after month, if necessary.

Then, instead of just hoping and praying that God will mysteriously drop it into your lap, what if you learned to ask—seek—and knock; ask—seek—and knock, until the door opened? What if this asking—seeking—and knocking was Jesus' secret code to blessing, victory, or clarity?

Think about it like this. Parents of sixteen year old, want-to-be-drivers understand this. I am one of those parents right now. Truth be told, you want your sixteen year old to learn how to drive. You want them to be able to enjoy the benefits and experience the opportunities that come with being able to drive. Yet, before the keys are handed over, you are grateful for driver's education. You are grateful for persistent, focused attention. You are even grateful that others will test them before licensing them.

What seems so unfair to a sixteen year old, who just wants you to hand them the keys, makes perfect sense to every parent. The blessing of unsupervised driving comes after driver's education, after lots and lots of practice, and after successfully passing their driving test. As great as driving is, no parent wants that blessing to be the tool that injures, maims, or kills their child.

Their persistent, focused attention develops both the understanding and the skill they will need to be successful drivers.

Why would we think God is any different? Before we can experience some of the freedoms and blessings we want, it might require some persistent, focused attention first.

Perhaps some of the blessings we want are things we are not yet ready to handle. Maybe some of the blessings we think we want are things God knows will not be good for us.

As hard as that seems to be to swallow, let me put it this way. Can you recall a time when you really wanted something to happen, but it did not? Maybe a job opportunity came and went or a potential date with someone came and went. At that time how did you feel? Disappointed? Angry? Let down? All of the above?

Let's say a few months or years pass and you discover some new information you didn't have when you first wanted that thing. Now that you have this new information, you pause and mentally say, "Wow, good thing that never happened after all!" Have you ever had an experience like that? If we are honest, all of us have. Some of us call it our twenty-year class reunion!

Sometimes the things we want are not the things we need the most. Asking, seeking, and knocking can bring clarity to this.

One other value behind asking, seeking, and knocking is that there are times during this process that our Heavenly Father wants to lead us to something even better than what we are considering at the moment. How good is that?

I could recount numerous stories of where this was the case in my life. Time spent asking, seeking, and knocking turned something good into something much better.

All that to say, there can be so much value in learning to ask, seek, and knock in one area of our lives until a breakthrough happens, clarity is given, or some new victory is experienced.

Most of us have many vague and varied desires. Many of them often show up as New Year's resolutions. In fact, they show up year after year after year. We want a lot of things. We focus a little time and effort on each one of them—at least for a while. When a miraculous breakthrough doesn't happen in our dating or married life, in our finances, in our health, or in some other area of need or interest, we tend to give up, blame God, or both.

Most of us know how difficult it is to focus on too many areas. Yet, we think the answer is to try harder, to pray more, to be more positive, more self-disciplined. What if the real problem is simply not picking one area to be absolutely committed to until a breakthrough happens? What if a lack of having one area (or the right area first) to focus on is the real problem?

I believe a key to getting what you want is allowing God to show you the one area that you need to give a disproportionate amount of time and attention to. We might say, "Manage other areas, but master this one." Ask, seek, knock; ask, seek, knock, until a door of blessing, victory, or clarity opens.

> **Manage other areas, but master this one.**

After it does, take another area and do the same, until that door opens too. In time, door after door after door will open because you finally understand Jesus' Secret Code.

Now this thought may be new to many of us, so in the final chapter I'll wrap up with a few practical insights on how you can put this code into practice in your daily life.

Secret Summaries

- Sometimes the things we want are not the things we need the most. Asking, seeking, and knocking can bring clarity to this.

- See yourself behind Door #2, in your secret place. Start by becoming intimately acquainted with who God is and what His kingdom is really like.

- Allow God to show you the *one* area that you need to give a disproportionate amount of time and attention to. We might say, "*Manage* other areas, but *master* this one." Ask, seek, knock; ask, seek, and knock until a door of blessing, victory, or clarity opens.

Valuable Action Step

Give some time every day to listen, learn, and receive what God wants to give you on that topic. Write down your insights and lessons. Act on what He brings to your mind. Manage other areas, but begin to master this one. There is a reward in doing this that can lead to new victories, growth, blessings, and significance that may not come any other way.

Be patient. This, like so many other skills we develop, takes time. Use the study guide at the end of this book to reinforce the ideas and principles.

FOCUS TIME

They were called stereograms. Do you know what that is? The first one I saw was in San Francisco, on Pier 39. A small crowd had gathered around what appeared to be a normal poster, sitting on an easel.

What caught my attention was not the poster but the people encouraging each other as they looked at the poster. It was actually more like coaching each other than encouraging.

"Just squint," one would say. "Gaze past the poster and relax your eyes," another would suggest. Every so often you would hear a, "I see it. I see it. It's really there!"

That's what drew me in. I'm a sucker for discovering new things. What was all the fuss? I had to see for myself.

I was told that these stereograms are computer-generated pictures within a picture. If you properly focus your eyes (or un-focus your eyes), a hidden image will come out at you in three-dimension.

I was also told IQ might be a factor. Well, now the pressure was on. Certainly, I am as smart as that lady jumping up and down saying, "I see them! I see them!"

I was told there were three dolphins in the picture. I really can't say, because I got a headache before they ever jumped out at me in 3D. After a few minutes of blurring, squinting, and crossing my eyes, I had to take their word for it. How humiliating to see but never really see.

I wish this lack of seeing was regulated to computer-generated images on five dollar posters. It is not. This "not seeing" problem is epidemic. The problem with that is this: what you don't see, can often limit you the most.

Failing to see dolphins in 3D didn't negatively affect my life (only my ego temporarily). Failing to see more important things can and does negatively affect us all the time.

- Many people who have been in car accidents often say they didn't see the other car. Not seeing was a real problem.
- People who have survived a heart attack often express how they had no idea their arteries were nearly blocked. Not seeing was a real problem.
- I've had both men and women come into my office after a spouse has left them. It's not uncommon for someone to say they didn't see it coming. Not seeing is a real problem.

Are we doomed to this kind of intermittent blindness? Is there a way to sharpen our focus?

As we discovered in the previous chapter, one of the things most of us fail to do is narrow our focus so that we concentrate extra time, energy, thought, and prayer on one area of our lives. We manage and maintain the other areas, while we seek to master this one. I call this my focus time.

> What you don't see can often limit you the most.

What I didn't tell you about my experience on Pier 39 was this. There were actually about a half a dozen of these stereograms. I would look at one for a few moments, and then try another and another and another. I spent about fifteen minutes working up that headache.

What I didn't notice, at the time, was that most of the people who ended up "seeing" spent all their time on one poster until they got it! What was even more impressive was that once they got one, they seemed to be able to, in mere seconds, see the image in each of the other posters.

Their focused approach allowed them to see many things my random approach failed to accomplish for me. I didn't lack desire, commitment, or IQ (I don't think). What I did lack was focus.

I say that because after about an hour of wandering around the pier (and after my headache had disappeared), I went back one more time to the stereograms. I had to give it one more try. Call it determination, a competitive spirit, or a bruised ego needing some reinforcement. Whatever it was, I was back.

It was during this second trip when I learned "the secret". The manager of the store gave it away. He said, "It might take ten minutes, but virtually everyone who picks one poster and stays with it, gets it. And once they get one, they generally can get all the rest in seconds."

That was my problem. It wasn't an IQ issue after all. Imagine my relief! I had failed to pick one poster and give it focused attention.

I'm proud to say, my poster turned out to be a very cool 3D image of the Golden Gate Bridge. Oh, the sweet feeling of success.

I wish that what I learned that day I would have applied to other areas of my life. Like most people, I had many desires and goals. I gave divided time and energy to each of them and gained only limited yardage on any. I didn't lack desire, self-discipline, or commitment. I lacked specific and bold persistence. I lacked understanding of Jesus' code. I lacked a focus time.

What if this is it? What if this will help you experience more victories, blessing, and clarity – but they come one open door at a time?

Jesus included this core principle at the end of the prayer we call the Lord's Prayer. In fact, when you study the passage (Luke 11:1-10), Jesus spent more time on the part I am calling the Secret Code than He spent on what we call the Lord's Prayer. That fact, by no means, suggests the Lord's Prayer is less important. But it should at least underscore how we cannot detach this second section from the previous one.

Many people have memorized the Lord's Prayer. Far fewer know that this asking, seeking, and knocking section is all part of the same lesson on prayer. One is really not complete without the other.

There is a prayer plan and there is a prayer focus. Both are parts of Jesus' Secret.

Let's review the Prayer Plan for a moment. It has three parts:

- **Worshiping**
- **Surrendering**
- **Receiving**

I determine a time and place to regularly slow down and connect with my Heavenly Father. In my case, I have literally set up a daily reminder in my Microsoft Outlook program (use whatever works best for you – a note card on a mirror is a common tool). My personality and lifestyle are like many of yours. Once the engines get roaring, unless I have a warning light flashing at me, I will likely slip into high gear and drive right through my entire day and miss this time.

For me, this daily pop up on my computer is a great tool to remind me of what I am aspiring to do.

Once there, I begin by reminding myself how big, great, holy, compassionate and generous He is.

Then, I once again surrender myself to His will. I remind myself that God knows what's best, better than I know what's best.

I open myself to receiving His forgiveness, power, and direction in my life. I do that as a simple outflow of remembering the kind of God He is. I know that when I have commitment to His will, I am in line for His blessing and help. I don't beg or plead during this time. In fact, I often make it an expression of gratitude for His gifts of forgiveness, wisdom, power, and blessing. There is nothing I can do to earn or deserve them. It's because of His character and love that they are available.

I then take time to listen. This is one of the most important spiritual habits any of us can develop. It is listening not with our physical ears, but our spiritual ear. God has given all of us a spiritual ear if we take time to learn how to use it.

If you have followed the lessons from the previous chapters, you have already set yourself up to overcome the two biggest barriers for not hearing the voice of God. They are "Busyness" and "Competing Agendas".

"Busyness" is simply not taking the time to listen. But if you create a secret place and time away from distractions, you will overcome this giant barrier.

"Competing Agendas" are the battle between your will and God's. But if you have already submitted your will to His and have put His kingdom plans ahead of your own, the second biggest barrier is also gone.

Like a child learning to walk, the rest of becoming a good listener will simply come through practice. Give it a try!

Here's something I do. I often say, "Lord, what is the next area You want me to give focused attention to?" Most of the time, it's not all that complicated to narrow it down to two, three, or four areas. They are areas of need or desire. They are areas that are causing us problems or areas of interest and desire we cannot shake.

Sometimes it is a habit that is holding us back and sometimes it is a blessing we long to experience or enjoy. Coming up with two, three, or four issues is not hard. What is hard is discerning which areas are going to be temporarily *maintained* and which one area is going to move to the top to be *focused* on and *mastered.*

The apostle Paul did this. He said, "I am focusing all my energies on this one thing: Forgetting the past and looking forward to what lies ahead" (Philippians 3:13).

Even if it takes several days or weeks to come to that decision, keep praying about it until you can't seem to shake the one area from your heart and mind. It may not be the one you want to work on first, but it's the one that God knows needs to be first. Win a victory here, get clarity here, and the other areas will be easier.

For example, some people want a financial breakthrough but they also have impulse issues that wreak havoc in their lives. Which do you think needs to be addressed first?

Some people really want to get married—they have a God-given desire to be married, but they also have serious self-defeating habits. Things like self-esteem issues, anger issues, alcohol or drug issues, or sexual impurity issues that battle within. Which do you think God will bring to the surface to deal with first—the desire or the need? I hope you said, "The need."

It's not that God can't or won't bless us until we get 100 percent of our issues resolved. It is just that most of us want the keys to the car before we are capable of driving responsibly. Some issues really need to be dealt with before we focus on getting one more blessing.

All of that to say: be patient to let the right area come to the top of your focus list.

Once I have determined the area, I again use my Outlook program and count out at least ninety days and enter "V-Day" (my victory or clarity day) into my calendar (a paper calendar can work just as well). This is not an exact day when completion is guaranteed; rather, it is a tangible reminder that I have a bunch of focus days in front of me. It is also a reminder that asking, seeking, and knocking in this one area won't go on indefinitely. Jesus did say, "The door would be opened!" (Matthew 7:7) Count on it.

Could this be it? What if a key aspect to Jesus' Secret is to spend some time every day on *one* area that needs specific and passionate persistence until a breakthrough occurs? What if that is the Secret Code to Door #1 and many, many blessings we would like to see come into our lives? What if it is one of the keys to being in the center of God's will?

Socrates said, "An unexamined life is not worth living." Most of us are generally so busy trying to get more, or so busy managing what our getting-more lifestyles have created, we don't take time to focus or examine where we really are going in life.

A "Focus Time" can change that.

Does this challenge you to look at goals differently? Desires differently? Prayer differently? It does me.

Instead of my focus being about getting what I think I want, my focus is getting clarity on (and making advances in) the one next thing I believe God wants me to do, become, or receive.

Door #1 is still the "get what I want" door, but what I want is now defined and directed by my Heavenly Father, who knows what I need much more than I know what I need.

This secret is revolutionizing my prayer life. I have learned more, grown more, and received more by following Jesus' plan and using Jesus' code than at any other time in my life. In fact, writing this book is not only an exploration of this topic, it is one of the outcomes of my focus time with Him.

Putting some of my teaching material in writing has been a goal of mine for years. It just wasn't happening very quickly.

With all my other personal and professional demands, where would I have the time?

But when I allowed the Lord to determine my focus time, everything began to change. When I allowed Him to define Door #1, allowed Him to define what I really wanted, and then focused on it until there was victory, clarity, or blessing, I then began to find time, energy, and insight I didn't have before.

One of the insights that came from my focus time was something that gave me a huge perspective change. It was a paradigm shift in an area most of us battle — the lack of time. The insight was this. What if, instead of having a lack of time, power, and resources, what if I have all the time and all the power to do everything God wants me to do, if I surrender to His will.

For me, that simple change of perspective began to bring about a wave of change downstream. Mostly, it began to reinforce how much I needed to be dialed into God's plan for me.

Instead of being worried and uptight about all the things I needed and wanted to do (or wanted to have), I began to seek what He wanted me to do and have. Instead of spending so much time and energy trying to get God to do want I wanted Him to do, I now spend time discovering what He wants to say to me about the one main area we are working on.

I *manage* the other areas, but one door at a time something new is being *mastered.* And just like those silly stereograms, it appears that once you've mastered one the other areas get easier. A success in one area gives wind to the sails in other areas.

This secret code is bringing new breakthroughs into my life that I hadn't experienced before. It is helping me to do what God is blessing instead of trying to get God to bless what I am doing.

In case you read right past that too quickly, let me repeat it: *Jesus' secret code can help us to focus on doing what God is blessing instead of trying to get God to bless what we are doing.*

That is huge!

But that's not all! An additional benefit to all this was time, the very thing I felt I was lacking the most. I discovered that when I gave God time, I got more time.

What if, behind Door #1, there are breakthroughs and blessings awaiting you too? I believe there are. I believe Jesus' Secret is for any and everyone who will follow it. There are spiritual, relational, financial, physical, emotional, and vocational breakthroughs that God wants you to experience.

I hope and pray you are one of those who will embrace Jesus' Secret. If you do, I know you will discover something much greater than merely getting what you want. Instead, you will discover the life your Heavenly Father created you for. You can discover what He wants you to receive, become, and do — one door at a time. Most importantly, you will discover a growing and authentic relationship with your Heavenly Father.

Jesus' Secret has been revealed to you. I hope and trust you too will be one who experiences firsthand how it is better than any other "secret" out there.

Let me leave you with one more spiritual declaration. Let this become a summation of Jesus' Secret Code:

You can discover what HE wants you to receive, become, and do – one door at a time.

**I daily give some focused time
to the one area God wants me to experience a
breakthrough in.**

Be willing to get alone with God long enough until this one area emerges? Then begin to give some time every day to listen, learn, and receive what God wants to give you on that topic. Write down your insights and lessons. Act on what He brings to your mind. Manage other areas, but begin to master this one. There is a reward in doing this that can lead to new victories, growth, blessings, and significance that may not come any other way.

Be patient. This, like so many other skills we develop, takes time. Use the study guide at the end of this book to reinforce the ideas and principles. Go back through the book to truly let Jesus' Secret sink in.

This book is not the end, but the beginning of a new adventure. If you will do it, you are about to embark on a great journey of discovery. You are about to discover in greater clarity than ever before the life you were created for.

With that in mind, let me end this section by offering you a prayer. Put yourself in this prayer. Make it as sincere and personal as you can.

Heavenly Father, I remind myself how big and great and holy and compassionate and generous You are. Your will and Your way is the only way to true life. I pray that You would open my eyes to see what you want me to see. May I find new power, insight, and blessing by being with You in secret. May You reveal the next area You want me to focus on. Give insight into what you want me to know, become, do, or receive. Let those insights transform me and bless me in brand new ways. Open new doors of victory and significance, one after the other. Let me come to know You more and Your great plan that You have for my life. I pray this in the powerful name of the One who gave us this secret, Jesus Christ, my Lord! Amen!

I look forward to hearing the amazing doors God opens for you!

www.JesusSecretBook.com

Spiritual Declaration #3:

I daily give some <u>focused</u> time to the <u>one</u> area God wants me to experience a breakthrough in.

Secret Summaries

- Listening to the still small voice of God is one of the most important spiritual habits I can develop. It is listening not with my physical ear, but my spiritual ear. God has given me a spiritual ear if I take time to learn how to use it.

- Instead of my focus being about "getting what I think I want," my focus is getting clarity on (and making advances in) the one next thing I believe God wants me to do, become, or receive.

- There are spiritual, relational, financial, physical, emotional, and vocational breakthroughs God wants me to experience.

- I can discover what He wants me to receive, become, and do — one door at a time. Most importantly, I can discover a growing and authentic relationship with my Heavenly Father.

Valuable Action Step

Even though your focus time is alone with God, that does not mean what you are learning or experiencing has to remain private. In fact, partnering with someone regarding your area of focus can be very valuable. Consider partnering up with one other person to discuss what you are doing and where you are feeling success or frustration. This is a grand adventure. Be willing to share with a few select people what you are experiencing in secret.

Go through the study guide at the end of this book with those people.

There's one more prayer I want to pray over you at the end of that.

My Spiritual Declarations

I will daily slow down for some private and personal
time with my Heavenly Father.

∞

I will discover the life I was created for by growing in
my worship of my Heavenly Father; surrendering, in
advance to His will; and receiving from Him all He
promises to give.

∞

I daily give some focused time
to the one area God wants me to experience a
breakthrough in.

My Daily Prayer Guide

WORSHIPING—I remind myself how big and great and holy and compassionate and generous You are (*our Father, hallowed be Your name*). As my Heavenly Father, You want to develop an intimate relationship with me.

SURRENDERING—Your will and way is the only way to true life and freedom (*Your kingdom come, Your will be done*). I remind myself that I have all the time and all the power to do everything You want me to do, as I surrender to Your will.

RECEIVING—I understand the kind of loving Heavenly Father You are, and the kinds of things You can do. I trust You with my basic needs and receive *all* that You have to give to me (*Give us this day our daily bread and forgive us …protect us*).

FOCUSING—I take You up on Your invitation to ask, seek, and knock regarding the next big area You want me to focus on. Help me to learn, do, or receive what You want regarding this area. I take time to listen. I commit at least the next ninety days to give focus time to this area.

Study Guide

One of the greatest ways to learn and grow is with others. Mutual sharing and camaraderie not only make the journey more exciting and interesting, we also tend to follow through better. Even though much of the application of this book is done in private, the discovery and dialog of it can be greatly enhanced in a group. Find one or two other people who will go through this with you.

The following questions can be explored individually, but are written with a small group in mind. They can reinforce the material throughout this book, as well as serve to bring greater clarity to Jesus' secret.

Enjoy the voyage!

Small Group Discussion and Questions – Part 1

In preparation for these questions, read or review chapters 1–3.

1. Prayer can be a challenging topic for anyone. What challenges, difficulties, or questions has it created for you?

2. Discuss the opening key life question. What difference could your answer to that question make in your life?

3. If life is really about discovering what I'm created for, more than about getting what I want, how might that affect your prayer life?

4. Read Mathew 6:5-8. What benefits do you think could come out of a secret time with God? What might be a reward? Have you experienced that?

5. Read Matthew 6:7-8. How does it affect you knowing that God cares more about a time and place with you than He does the exact words you use or don't use?

6. Do you have a favorite secret place and time to connect with God? If so, why have you chosen that time/place?

Valuable Action Step

If you don't have a specific place and time to get alone with your Heavenly Father, make plans today to do that. Pick a place and determine what time you will show up there tomorrow. Like any other important event, put it on your calendar. Do this every day for the next ninety days. Determine one day in advance when the best time will be to show up there tomorrow. Start off with just ten minutes and let it grow and develop from there.

Small Group Discussion and Questions - Part 2

In preparation for these questions read or review chapter 4.

1. Read Matthew 6:5-13. Share something that stands out to you, helps you, or challenges you about this passage.

2. All of us want to receive from God, but Jesus begins the Lord's Prayer with worship and surrender. Why do you think many people leave out (or under-develop) what amounts to two-thirds of true prayer? How might neglecting those two areas negatively affect us?

3. What do you think growing in worship could do for a person's relationship with God? Discuss some ideas of how a person could grow in worship and increase their awareness of who God is?

4. In what practical ways could surrendering to God's will show up in a given week or month?

5. If there is an area of surrender you committed to in the past, and are free to share it, tell what you did, and how it affected you.

6. Often, when we talk or think about God's plan for our lives, we think about the whole plan. What does Psalm 37:23 reveal about how God directs us or how much He reveals? How does that affect your thinking on this topic?

Valuable Action Step

Spiritual declarations cannot only be great reminders of what we have learned, but more importantly, they can begin to focus where we want to go. We move toward what we daily focus on. Copy or tear out the "Spiritual Declarations" page (page 145). Hang it on the mirror you use to get ready in the morning. Recite the declarations out loud. Commit them to memory. Breakthrough behavior requires breakthrough beliefs. These declarations can help that to happen.

Small Group Discussion and Questions - Part 3

In preparation for these questions read or review chapter 5.

1. Read Luke 11:1-10. Jesus concludes the Lord's Prayer with a parable. The story shows how one guy with a persistent focus had a door opened to him. Jesus ends by telling us to ask, seek, and knock so doors would open to us. How does this parable and principle challenge your idea of prayer?

2. Part of the secret of asking, seeking, and knocking involves time for us to get clarity on a topic. Often, we can want things that aren't good for us or will take us in a direction that causes us to miss out on the best. Can you think about a time when you didn't get something (or someone—a date perhaps) only to later breathe a sigh of relief? What does that tell you about our limited perspective?

3. Most of us can easily come up with at least three or four things we would like to see happen in our lives. Narrowing it down to the *one next* thing to focus on is key. Listening for the still small voice of God becomes essential. What are some ways that might help you develop your spiritual listening?

Valuable Action Step

Even though your focus time is alone with God, that does not mean what you are learning or experiencing has to remain private. In fact, partnering with someone regarding your area of focus can be very valuable. Consider partnering with one other person to discuss what you are doing and where you are feeling success or frustration. This is a grand adventure. Be willing to share with a few select people what you are experiencing in secret.

Small Group Discussion and Questions
– Part 4

In preparation for these questions read or review chapter 6.

1. Share your own stereogram experience of not being able to see what was right in front of you.

2. Something can be in front of our eyes, yet if we fail to give proper focus, we don't really see. Share some practical steps you are considering to help you in your focus time.

3. The apostle Paul said, "I am focusing all my energies on this *one thing*: Forgetting the past and looking forward to what lies ahead" (Philippians 3:13). What do you think he is referring to when he mentions, "forgetting the past"? Why would that be important in his current focus time?

4. All of us have mental messages that we repeat over and over. Some of them can sabotage our current progress now. What are some examples of mental files that could hold someone back from receiving the victory or blessing God wants to give them through their focus time?

Valuable Action Step

Determine how to record what you are hearing or learning from your focus time—or hope to hear or learn from your focus time. Do you need to buy a journal? Do you need to open a Word document and call it "My Focus Time"? Setting up the practical side of this time is a key action step. Be willing to explore what works best for you. Do your best to record at least one thing every day for the next ninety days.

CONGRATULATIONS!

If you are reading this page, let me congratulate you! You are on your way to many open doors of victory, blessing, and significance.

Let me conclude with one final prayer that the apostle Paul first prayed. I humbly offer these as words from one growing sojourner to another.

I pray that from his glorious, unlimited resources he will give you mighty inner strength through his Holy Spirit. And I pray that Christ will be more and more at home in your hearts as you trust in him. May your roots go down deep into the soil of God's marvelous love. And may you have the power to understand, as all God's people should, how wide, how long, how high, and how deep his love really is. May you experience the love of Christ, though it is so great you will never fully understand it. Then you will be filled with the fullness of life and power that comes from God. Now glory be to God! By his mighty power at work within us, he is able to accomplish infinitely more than we would ever dare to ask or hope. May he be given glory in the church and in Christ Jesus forever and ever through endless ages. Amen (Ephesians 3:16-21 NLT).

Printed in the United States
105059LV00002B/280-999/P

9 781604 774788